REFLECTIONS

A WOMAN'S JOURNEY THROUGH LIFE EXPERIENCES

ANNIE K. KOSHI

outskirtspress
DENVER, COLORADO

Outskirts Press, Inc.
http://www.outskirtspress.com

ISBN: 978-1-4327-8413-3

Library of Congress Control Number: 2011962172

Outskirts Press and the "OP" logo are trademarks belonging to Outskirts Press, Inc.

PRINTED IN THE UNITED STATES OF AMERICA

Special thanks to Mr. Robert Ackerson, who coordinates Riverdale Senior Center Poetry Group, New York City, the source of inspiration for some of the poems in this collection.

Contents

SECTION XIII

ON *Young Indian-Americans*

SECTION XIV

ON *My Old Story*

To My Readers

Reflections is a collection of poems I have been writing over the years. They are mostly disclosures and confessions related to my life story—a heroic story of living with emotional pain without surrendering, and always fighting to win and succeed. I don't claim that my story is unique in any way. It could be the story of many of those who read my poems. For some of you readers, *Reflections* could give you flashbacks into your own fight to succeed, despite numerous hurdles on the way, and could give you some inspiration to write your own story in poetry or prose; for some others, it could be some "starlight" to follow and be guided through.

Section I, "On Being Born Female and Dark Skinned," reflects my inner conflict resulting from being judged and derogated on the ground of my skin complexion. By the way, color prejudice is not a "white man's invention" used against the Black race. It exists intra-racially in some Hispanic and most South Asian societies, where women are discriminated against, based on miniscule differences in skin tone, for example, dark brown, wheat brown, and the like. However, these women may not face discrimination in professional and business fields, as in many Western countries.

Except for the poem "Color Power," written in light of color discrimination I was subjected to in the United States in my professional field, all poems in this section are reflective of the arranged marriage system and its culturally prevalent corollary, the dowry system in India, where I was born and where I grew up, until I came to the United States for my graduate studies. These poems reflect the pitiable, deplorable plight any girl/woman who has gone or is going through similar disparaging situations in any similar society.

Readers might resent my bitter poetic voice in some of these lines, especially those related to the male gender, but you, men, please understand that I am just ranting at the rotten social mores, using my "poetic license." I understand that in one way, not just women, but men too, get caught in the web of social evils.

The last five poems in this section are put in generalized terms. The one titled "When She Rings the Doorbell" is reflective of the ill treatments many women in many parts of even this modern world receive. The message in the next poem, "Ageless Beauty," is that a woman's beauty is not manifested in skin color or chronological age, but is internal and personality-related. In "Prayer to Stars," I am metaphorically applying the philosophy of gender equality to the stars in the sky, praying to the Day Star, the Sun, not to outshine the soft-white light of the night stars, namely, Queen Moon and her retinue, the little stars, since both are of equal worth to Mother Earth. The last two poems are addressed to both men and women. The message in the ending chant poem with an "Obamaean" overtone is that the ball of change lies in both men's and women's courts alike, and both have the option to pick it up, play, and win the game of change, the only rule being openness.

Once you follow me through the rest of the pages, you will begin to look at me not as a radical feminist but as a noble fighter, who conquered angry, resentful emotions with true passion for living a successful life.

Section II is in honor of all mothers, whose love and sacrifice have been the power sources providing vital energy to the world's greatest men and women of all times. I bow in high obeisance to all mothers, including me—both biological and non-biological.

Section III is a disclosure of the origin of my tragic saga and my philosophy of living it. Many of you may have comparable stories to tell.

In Section IV, you will witness the struggles I have gone through and how I got metamorphosed into a hopeful life with a rewarding future to look forward to, be it short or long. I've found forgiving the best antidote to soothe and heal hurtful wounds.

In Section V, I am sharing my data bank of some facts of life on various topics, stored and saved from experience and retrieved by my muse. Hopefully, you will find commonalities you agree with.

Section VI is in celebration of a keepsake I treasure, and which is symbolic of my cherished desire to climb the social ladder of the academy as a foreign student in the United States with very limited financial backup.

In Section VII, you will know me as a nature lover. The apartment I live in faces the Hudson River, which gives me plenty of opportunities to watch, enjoy, and reflect on nature's beauty that comes with the change of seasons.

In Section VIII, I am talking to and about angels, whose existence up in heaven and their occasional visits to humans as testified in two sacred books, namely, the Bible and the Qur'an, remain a mystery to me, and probably to many of you. I wonder if some day I could be visited by one of them for the mystery to be unraveled!

The loss grieved at in Section IX, I am sure, is not much different from what some of you have suffered at some time in your life.

Section X "celebrates" an unusual loss; that of a very young lady, an "early bloomer" in her adopted land, and whom the terrorists shamelessly caused to be burned in flames and smoke—one of thousands of 9/11 victims.

In Section XI, I very proudly express my admiration and appreciation of the limitless opportunities the United States, my adopted country, made up of immigrants from different parts of the world, offers to all and sundry, irrespective of any kind of apparent handicaps.

In Section XII, I pay homage to the builders of the Indian-American society in the U.S., which I am proud to be a member of, and whose pioneering hard labor has made them one of the most economically thriving ethnic groups in the U.S.

Section XIII is my plea to young Indian-American citizens to listen to my "Longfellowian" voice, which tells them how to build their ship of American future and have it set sail, wrestling successfully with "waves and whirlwinds," as I have been doing all through my life.

By the time you finish reading the last section (XIV), you would have known me as I am now and how I reached this stage of equanimity and balance. Hopefully, during your journey of reading through these poems, some of you must have "discovered" yourself, because you have a similar story to tell. Don't you want to share?

SECTION I

On Being Born Female and Dark Skinned

1. Dark Fetus

The skies were blue,
not all the stars shining, though.
A single star so dark
shone through silver clouds
when Mom and Dad
MADE LOVE

on a roomy bed lit with
silk-shaded oil lamp
dimmed and calmed by
white walls
on all four sides.

Bamboo mats, woven
white and soft,
spread so neatly on
the lovers' red mahogany bed.

Lily-white robes and
soft-white cotton sheets
to cover, if needed.

Perfect whiteness for pure
white lovemaking.

White moonlight, bright and brave,
not darkened whatsoever,
peeks in through
the peephole dark and white
just to bless the lovers' make.

Moony, starry, peaceful night,
the moon so white, the star so dark.
Star so made to power and rule
the fate of fetus dark
born in Perfect Whiteness.

Is it true
stars make your fate?

Do gods and stars conspire
against the aspirant fruit of love
to be gendered and endangered,
and wilted by color codes?

2. Born Dark Starred

She was not born on
a lucky star. Dark
clouds enshrouded her star
when her mother went
into labor; no wonder she
was born dark starred.

Darkness followed her
ever since. A dark cloud
surfaced her skin, making
her dark skinned.

"Your skin makes you look ugly,
you, the undesired girl.
No guys will ever desire you,
you, dark skinned, rough skinned."

"Go to a nunnery,
hide your skin in white robes
as nuns do. Never mind, the robes
won't hide your dark face."

With no choice but to listen to,
follow up on, her folks' voice
internalized, built into
her growth hormone,

out she went in search of love.
Little did she know
nuns had color codes too.

3. Dark Baby Girl

The little girl in my village
was born dark
into the dark world.

Dark was the village,
and still is.
Baby girl is dark,
groan the village folks.

Born dark
with no market
or sale in marriage!

Darkie, sweetie,
cutie, beauty,
Mommy sings.

Costly is this sweetie,
Daddy cries.

Dark was the village,
and still is.
Baby girl is dark,
groan the village folks.

Camouflage is the trick,
say the village folks.

Bleach her skin,
dust it with talcum.
Adorn her neck
with white pearls
and wrists
in shiny gold bracelets.

Dark was the village,
and still is.
Baby girl is dark,
groan the village folks.

Daddy's thoughts are wild,
Mommy's love is mild.

Dark or fair,
my girl
IS
my labor's fruit fare.

Dark was the village,
and still is.
Baby girl is dark,
groan the village folks.

Mommy sings aloud,
groans so loud.

Are all the angels white?
Are all the saints fair?
No dark angels above?
No black, no dark saints?

My girl is an angel,
my girl is a saint,
Mommy sings to her angel.

Dark was the village,
and still is.
Baby girl is dark,
groan the village folks.

Daddy's shrieks rise above.
Nature made an error
and I made a blunder
when I made love.

Why couldn't she be a boy?
Who can change her gender
now and forever,
so I get the dowry for the boy?

4. Dark Blossom

Dark blossom is blooming.
Full womanhood,
sensuous bosom,
perfect biology.

Dark blossom is sappy
oozing sap so timely
with clocklike accuracy
fertile for "insemenation."[1]

Dark blossom is blooming
for surgeon male
who sees power
in color biology.

Dark blossom is braving
surgical codes
that bifurcate the epidermis
surgeon male buys to cut.

Dark blossom is savvy,
knows for sure
fair skin "insemenation" is
free,
dark skin "insemenation" is
money.

1. This has a different connotation from "insemination."

Loud is the query,
the challenge:

Does your biology
or your chemistry
sense the power
of skin and money
when you copulate?

5. Dark Lady

Is she the moon of dark clouds,
or the sun of bright blue sky?
Difficult to tell
'cause her skin is dark.

Is she tanned by the sun,
burned by fire,
browned by smoke?
Difficult to tell from her skin.

Could she be exciting?
Arousing and appetizing?
Difficult to tell
'cause she's dark.

Is she luscious?
Sensuous and virtuous, too?
Difficult to tell
'cause of her dark skin.

Could she be the taste of his kiss,
the sweet sugar of his wild desires?
Difficult to tell
'cause her face is shining dark.

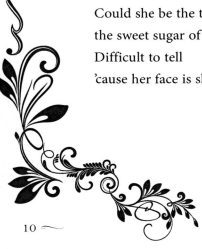

Is she sappy, seepy,
silky, spicy, saucy?

Difficult to feel
'cause of her dark covering.

Are her apples round and firm,
her raisins sweet to taste?
Difficult to tell
'cause our world is dark.

And to this our dark world
she is just a dark rind.

6. Dark Nobody

Dark Nobody
is Somebody.

Self-image brainwashed,
sails torn and twisted,
she steers hard,
searching for a lifeguard.

In the world
of fair men and women
she flounders
rudderless, de-sexed.

Should she row
the "ocean-craft" herself?
Or share one
rowed by a male?

Decision! She has
built up the woman-craft
and the womanpower
to row and man her world.

Look! She's wading
through strong, muscular
waves and winds,
with no spirit lost.

Nothing counts for her
but the heavy strokes
made light and bright
by her strong will-power.

Gravitational pull!
Uplifted bosom!
Elevated spirit!

Survival skills!
Powerful resistance!
Self-guided assistance!
Laudable persistence!
Noble existence!

7. Color Code

Bride
should be fair.
Groom
could be dark,
so says the social code.

The male has
no color,
no code.

Such is the code.
And color is the power
that rules my world.

To be female
and dark
is to be cursed
of the womb.

Such is the code.
And color is the power
that rules my world.

Fair or dark,
he is the
blessed of the womb.

Such is the code.
And color is the power
that rules my world.

8. Coffee Beans

Coffee beans with solid rind
and shiny seeds
are on the market
for bid.

Not so priced as wheat
or barley grains;
being of less value
to men buyers.

Donors pay the high cost
to make up the color
and texture
buyers look for.

Don't you want to deplore
your social mores
made of shades
of skin tone differences?

Colors make the spectrum
not on the layers
but deep inside
when the sun penetrates.

Doors are meant for protection
and sometimes for decoration.
Step inside to find
the color you want to find.

Seeds hide inside,
not open outside.
Peel off, feel in, find
the color deep, not the rind.

9. Surface Love

Your skin should be fair,
wheaten or peeled banana color
to be a commodity
of commercial value.

Is men's love on the surface?
Surface love
with no penetration
beyond the veneration
of the surface glove?

10. Male Power

Her bosom blooms
into full blossoms.

Sensuous bosom,
perfect biological bloom.

For surgeon male, not an attraction,
having his own code of bifurcation
applied with discrimination
against the dermis under investigation.

Fair skin operation
brings in freebies for the female,
status and class for the male.
No reasoning in calculation.

Dark skin operating power
has value in the money market,
despite no purchasing power
in the open market.

Dark skin operation is costly,
ironic though the male bargaining power
that goes up and up every hour.

The darker the female, the higher goes
the male bidding power.

Dark skin wins male power
if it comes with money power.

Male wins power.
Female wins color.

Pray for the world to change.
Pray for color power to change.
Pray for male power to change
while colors stay with no change.

11. Womb Power

Did Mom's womb
change color,
bearing me?
Or my brother?

Does the womb know
the code
the male world has made?

Womb stays female
for all eternity,
bearing both male
AND FEMALE.

COLORLESS STAYS
THE WOMB.
POWERFUL STAYS
THE WOMB.

You womb-less powers!
Womb was your abode,
your code,
your life,
your color.

Saints
know no colors.
Saints
know no genders.
Saintly
are the WOMBS.

Can we change the code?
Change the male?
Change the color
that made my world's code?

Use your womb power,
your female power.

Fight to change the code
made for the female
by the male.

12. Color Power

Color King,
Color Power, Power Color.

King in three names.
Corrupter, Deceiver, Hypocrite.

How dare you still reign
in my world of democracy,
still winning hearts,
ruining minds,
cheating kinds?

Your name is legion,
your dame, pollution,
your home, any religion,
your dome, all and every region.

You burn my profession
and doom my vocation.

Magician, Chameleon!
your colors are infinite.

Ghost!
Your entry is light.
Your might is my plight.

Multicolored, multicoated,
multilingual, multicultural,
cultured, civilized.

Reformer, color former,
you polarize, connive, divide.

Colored as I am
no less, no more.

I am
not a pawn
in your hands
rated, hated, or fated.

Souls know no color.
Nor is the air
we breathe in
white or black,
brown or yellow.

I see the same flame
from sun, moon, stars

burning all day and night
with equal distribution,
with no discrimination,
on all Mother Earth's children.

13. Ageless Beauty

I am abstract, so you can't name me.
I am inside, so you can't see me.
I am silent, so you can't hear me.
I am feeling, so you can't touch me.

I am thoughts, so you can't find words for me.
I am freedom, so you can't enslave me.
I am wisdom, so you can't fool me.
I am power, so you can't conquer me.

I am honest, you can confide in me.
I am truth, you can trust me.
I am open book, you can read me.
I am forgiving, you can approach me.

I am joy, you can enjoy me.
I am compassionate, you can feel me.
I am warm, you can embrace me.
I am love, you can adore me.

I am not made-up, so you can see through me,
not pretentious, so you can rely on me.
When I smile, I don't beguile.
Before I open my mouth, I think awhile.

My words aren't mean or crude.
My thoughts aren't unkind or rude.

I don't act in revenge,
not wanting to avenge.

Celebrities and pop stars are not my models.
I do not trust those ever-changing models.
I make my own models,
searching my own heart for ideals.

Touching, passionate hearts are my abode.
Warm, caring hands are my strong-hold.

Now let me uncover my face
for you to behold my touching eyes,
my skin's eyes, my heart's eyes,
my mind's eyes, my brain's eyes.

Look at me with unclouded eyes,
untainted, untinted eyes.

My name is
AGELESS BEAUTY.

14. When She Rings the Doorbell

She's the mother of passions,
of ambitions and aspirations,
of missions, long-term visions,
dreamed and un-dreamed.

She's the mother of labors,
tense, with no chance to relax,
trying to move mountains
with faith, hope, and love.

She's the mother of all the voice
despised, denigrated, segregated.

She's been indentured, enslaved,
whipped by masters,
clothed in shabby outfits,
and fed with husk and tasks.

She's known concentration camps,
outlived Auschwitz.

She
aspires to climb the Everest
with Hillary and Norgay,
to be on the winning climbers' list,
to be the best of best;

tries hard to make treaties
with her users and abusers
with pain at heart,
not losing hope in the least;

tries to carve homes out of mess,
build castles and pyramids
with kings and queens;

prays and wishes
her patient suffering be rewarded,
the heavens open up all the doors
when she rings the doorbell.

15. Prayer to Stars

The balmy night stars on the sky!
Queen Moon and her retinue
on the night sky!

Why are you so shy
when the King Sun comes out
on the daylight sky?

Don't you live in the same space as high
as the king's own mountain high?

I am the planet down below.
I live miles away
from where you, the Big Mighty Day Star
and the Moon Star with many a twinkling star
dwell so far away.

I am of humble birth, dwelling far below.
Dust and dirt are my foot-bed below,
while your feet walk on the spotless sky above.
With my big eyes always turned above,
I look at you, day and night from below.

I like you all, all you, stars,
both day and night stars,
since you both count for me.
Day and night equally count for me.

I need the Big Star's heat.
I need its hot energy all day long to meet
my need to have my children flourish,
animate and inanimate to equally flourish,
since not my desire that they ever perish.

I need the night stars' cool,
the moon's cool, the little stars' cool,
so soft as the cashmere blanket wool,

for my children to swim in their night pool,
their souls shining against the dark cool
and the seas' shimmering cool,
when your light falls on waves so cool.

❧❧

I pray
all you stars collaborate.
I can very well mediate.

I want my children to live in congruence
with all the stars in fair balance.

I pray
The Mighty Star's incandescent, aggressive heat
not outshine the night stars' soothing heat
just to keep the celestial kingdom in equilibrium
for my children down below to emulate.

16. Come Closer to Me

Come closer to me,
feel my heart beat
the same as yours.

My skin might look different,
I might belong to a different race.
Still we have the same soul,

the same spirit
of the same parent,
shared equally
with equal division, too;

the same perfect body combination
made of all the same elements
in the same miraculous mixture;

devised by the same potter
in the same old-fashioned way
with the same clay and water,
with the same chemical reaction,
in the same combination;

with the same built-in parts,
all working in unison
to produce and reproduce
the same power and energy

for equal transmission,
with no discrimination.

Red, brown, black, yellow, white,
dark chocolate, brown chocolate,
milk chocolate, wheat chocolate.

Despite all the different
shades of color and tone,
don't we have the same flesh
and blood combination?

Isn't the globe we inhabit
and inherit
the one and the same to merit?

Isn't what we breathe
in and out to be alive
the same air?

Don't we bleed
the same color blood
from our same pound of flesh?

Don't we all have
the same membership
in the same rich HUMAN family?

Don't we all have
the same last name?
Mankind?

Let's empty our hearts and minds,
throwing out into the trash
the different differences.

Let's hold hands together,
meditate together
on the same sameness
with hearts centered on
the same flame
burning all day and night
to illuminate the same Mankind.

Walk me to your prayer hall.
I want to pray with you all,
say the same prayer for us all.

We'll sing the same hymn
of our oneness.

17. Change the Dye

We can change; yes, we can.
You can change; yes, you can.
I can change; yes, I can.

Can colors mix and match? Yes, they can.
Can you mix and match? Yes, you can.
Can I mix and match? Yes, I can.
Do we want to? Yes and No.

Can dyes change colors? Yes, they can.
Can colors change the dyes? No, they can't.
Can we change our dye? Yes, we can.
Can we change our colored world? Yes, we can.

All the world is colors.
All the colors, its stage.
All the dyes, its players.

Oh, the Magician Dye!
You can perform. Yes, you can.
You can transform. Yes, you can.
You can trans-race. Yes, you can.
You can trans-color. Yes, you can.

My long-term wish
and prayerful cry!

Change the dye.
See my Color Perfect.

Can you change? Yes, you can.
Can I change? Yes, I can.

We can change; yes, we can.

SECTION II

On Motherhood

18. Mother Power

Mother!
Borne of mother,
born to mother,
born mother.

Mother!
Of kings and queens,
of pearls and earls,
of saints and angels,
of gods and goddesses.

Love!
Born of love,
born to love,
born love.

Milk!
Born of milk,
born to milk,
born milk.

Blossom!
Born to bloom,
never to fade,
and ever to shade.

Fruit!
Born to nourish
and cherish,
never to perish.

Your heart is all energy,
your arms so warm,
your bosom so overflowing
with love so patient, persistent.

Your power is
strength for world powers;
support, source, and resource.

19. Mother: Three in One

Mother, housewife, caretaker,
redeemer, consoler, comforter,

Three in One.

overworked, over-burdened,
unconditional, undivided,
manned, but unmanned.

One Ship, One Sail, One Captain.

Bright, warm, soothing;
fair, powerful, spirited;

One Sun, One Moon, One Sky.

Moaning, praying, craving;
showering, sprouting, pouring;

One River, One Shower, one Fountain.

Sensitive, sensuous, romantic;
thunderous, stormy, volcanic;

One Soul, One Spirit, One Energy.
One Lamb, one Pyre, one Urn.

Sacrificial meal, burning sati,[1]
flowing Ganges[2]
Very seldom solemnized
or acknowledged,
not rewarded, mostly victimized.

Trinity, Unity, Divinity!
Missionary, Visionary, Intermediary!

1. Sati, which used to be practiced in ancient India, requires the widow to burn
    herself in the same pyre as her dead husband's. Even though legally abolished in
    democratic India, it could continue to exist in some rural areas.
2. The Ganges (Ganga) is the most sacred river in India. Believed by many
    worshipers to be descended from heaven to earth, she is looked at as a vehicle
    of ascent from earth to heaven. She is worshiped as the mother who accepts
    and forgives all, as symbolized by the ritualistic bathing, which devotees do for
    purification of spiritual dirt.

SECTION III

On Vanished Vs. Remained

20. Living with Those Who Remained

My mom vanished for all eternity.
Totally from my babyhood life,
not even shades of memories left
to recall, to help face with sanity
my confused, turbulent life.

A cruel stroke of fate,
a never-to-be-refilled
vacuum to grow up with,
demanding survival skills
to develop and play with.

My mom, a sweet, beautiful lady,
as I am told,
got nipped in the bud
in God's own divine plan.

A natural death
at the prime age of twenty-two,
leaving back two half-orphaned treasures.
My brother, and myself, a cradle baby.

All my mom's dreams vanished
into the thin air
as she flew up into the sky,
melting into the clouds
never to return.
Not even visitation rights granted!

Pa remained with
custodial rights inherited,
trying to care and love.

Paternal grandma had
already been vanished,
a natural death on her middle way.
Paternal grandpa remained,
the patriarchal head.

Maternal hands vanished;
paternal hands remained.

Call it irony, destiny, providence,
bad luck, astrological star,
or whatever...

ingrained before being born,
never-to-be-erased DNA lines
born with, to put up with.

No choice but
to move on, go on,
not with thoughts of
whoever vanished,
who never would reappear,

but with those who remained
and with words and actions of
whomever substitutes you get
by design or fate,
hurts and wounds withstanding.

More so if you're born female!

No possible replacement surgery,
no implants, either,
to fill the holes
left by the vanished

except positive thinking,
the intra-venous fluid
for emotional invigoration.

Ambitious, hopeful wishes,
the blood transfusion
for the harmed heart
to gather momentum, restart
for revival, for transmutation.

SECTION IV

On Facing Up to Hurdles of Life

21. Anger and Me

Anger used to hurt me,
making me scream
with emotional pain,
lose control, blow up,

mad panic, throw tantrums,
do stupid things,
even try to kill myself,

just to take revenge on those
unfair, discriminatory folks
who caused me suffering
by their unacceptable behavior
and unfair, unjust actions.

I passed through
different stages of life,
taking up challenges,
but carried anger, the dynamite
lodged inside me,
prone to explode when triggered,

only to expose my weakness,
my lack of power and control
over my game of life
which only I could win.

Anger lurked in me for a long time,
tried to ruin my life
injecting burning poison
into my veins and arteries,

making me memorize
my past bleeding wounds.

❧

Now that I have reached
the land of mature age,
crossing bridges
of innumerable suffering,

putting my survival skills
to the best use
and am reaping
the hard-earned harvest
of my consistent,
persistent toil,

I talk to myself in calm.
to make sure anger, the evil spirit,
doesn't come out from its resort,
my aching heart.

22. My Blizzards of Life

My blizzards of life arrived roaring
with strong, stormy, cold winds
testing my resistance power,
gauging my tolerance level.

White snow surrounded me,
dazzling light blinded me,
though the sun wasn't shining,
not set either, so ironic.

Two contrasting colors reflecting,
dark and bright conflicting.

Icy snowballs hovered around,
pelting my heart's closed windows,
pushing hard and wild,
forcing them to open all around,

pressing me to feel with sorrows
the freezing cold that surrounds
the wild, unfair world around.

Puzzled, agonized, lost!
Surrender or fight?

Surrendering is humiliating,
fighting is tough, tight, tiring.

No escape from life's blizzards
of confusion, suffering, failures,
rejections, disappointments,
and countless lists of negatives
that make up all the blizzards.

Not wanting to stay
with all the icy mess
that blizzards leave to stay
in my heart's stress,

I tried not to delay
the cleaning up,
struggling though,
to do it fast,

hoping, wishing, praying
for a better tomorrow
to arrive fast
with no relay.

Wishful prayers always helped,
soothed my storm-swept mind,
heralding calm and peace
with balmy quiet.

23. My Music

My music was my tearful song,
my distressed song,
my mourning morning song,
my unsung evening song,
my dreary, weary, night song.

I was musical, though not singing,
having my own rhythmic music.
Not free to express in singing,
being oppressed by suppressed music.

My music was my cry for help,
wanting a confidante, kind and loving,
able to read my mind and help me
feel homey at home,
not to stay with unsung suffering.

Seeing no rainbow in the sky,
no sunlit sky, no moonlit sky,
I rode the surf so unruly,
hid myself in caves so gloomy.

My music became just sounds,
heard as rebel sticks and mutinous hands
beating the drums to make crazy noise
with no rhythmic beats, no control, no poise.

My music was a foreign language test,
not making my folks feel what I felt,
not understood, but put to the test,
an unwritten test, a wrap-around belt.

With my own music in my brain,
with no cheery instrumental music,
I made my own background music.

Agonized cries of music
with restrained refrain!

The music I composed made me wear
strange attires with all questions,
no answers, all whisper;
helped cover up wounds, not tear.

Deliverance so clever!

The music I made in my head was freedom,
The music I made in my brain was wisdom.
The music I made in my heart helped feel warm
not to storm, but to conform and transform.

24. My Life of Anticipation

Tomorrows used to frighten me,
scarecrows scaring at me.

Insecure of what to anticipate,
today being a theme to meditate
on what to make of tomorrow,
I lost both today and tomorrow,

not realizing how equally treasured
they both are and should be.

my cop-out voice whispered:
anticipate the worst for tomorrow
for not to have an upsetting tomorrow
if it turns out to be the worst.

You anticipated the worst,
so why worry about the worst?
Face it with courage, if you don't
want to get lost.

Didn't you lose your today
anticipating the worst tomorrow?

With mature age and wisdom gained,
my philosophy has changed.

Today is your past, by the time
you live your tomorrow.
Cherish the given today
leave for time
the uncertain tomorrow.

No anticipation can change tomorrow.
Wait for the experience of tomorrow
learned from the lessons of today,
from the realities of living today.

Things are inevitable to happen.
Anticipation won't bring in change.
though change is bound to happen
if you will and channel the change.

25. My Life of Hope

Hope is the warrior
who fights for me,
no matter I fail.

His long, strong rope
always outstretched for me
to clutch, to hold on,

beckoning me to climb mountains,
surmount competitions,
conflicts, rivalries,
confrontations, fights and feuds,

and always patrolling me
until I reach the peak.

Hope, my psychiatrist, my psychologist,
my counselor, my service manager,
my tour guide, my tour director,
my travel companion, my roommate,
my better half, my life partner!

You make me dream of tomorrow,
not wanting me to dig out
the dead yesterday.

Hope, you dwell in me
in different names;

courage, valor, acceptance,
perseverance, persistence,
determination, expectation,
positivity, creativity.

You assume multi-colors
and shades, no shadows;
all the rainbow colors,
shiny, shimmery, glittery.

You take different shapes;
full moon, crescent moon,
dazzling rising sun,
peaceful setting sun.

Hope, you sow your seeds in my soil,
prompting me to nurture
and nourish you for
my own growth and advancement.

You make me carry you
carefully wrapped up
in my fleece security blanket
to keep me warm and protected,
not deserted in the desert.

I travel miles and miles with you,
sowing your seeds on the way,
never wanting to look down below
at the dirt where they
fall and grow below.

You always prompt me to look up,
flying your seeds into the air,
knowing for sure
they hit the ground, no matter what.

I try not to look back to see
if they grow or die; no query.

They might grow into beautiful plants
with blossoming, fragrant flowers,
or into barren shrubs and forests
or even thorny bushes.

I strive to move on and on and on,
wandering, but carrying the covenant[1]

1. Metaphorical reference to the covenant God made with Abraham that he and his
   descendants (the Israelites) would be given the land of Canaan (Gen. 12:4-7,
   15:17-18; Exod. 13:11[King James & New American Bible Versions]).

between you and me
until I reach Sinai,[2]
the Canaan[2] of milk and honey,
never, never, never to look back
lest I become Sara's Pillar of Salt.[3]

৵৻৵

After Good Friday comes
The Resurrection Sunday,
The Easter Sunday.

2. Refers to the camp the Israelites set up on Mount Sinai (Exod. 19:1-2
[KJ&NAB]).

3. A biblical reference to Lot's (Abraham's nephew) wife, Sara, who became a
pillar of salt when she disobeyed God's instruction to run away to the hills
without looking back, in order to be saved from the burnt cities of Sodom and
Gomorrah (Gen.19:15–26 [KJ&NAB]). Here the reference is used to imply
that dwelling on the past might bring in only miseries.

26. My Winter

I am in the winter of my life, my summer life.
The clock reversed my winter into the summer.

I never have had a summer in my life
my summer was my winter,
now my winter, my summer.

My winter life is summery, not stormy, not cold.
Warm love burns hot inside, melting the winter cold
in my icy heart hardened with dreams shattered,
love unseen, unfulfilled, unrealized, unshared.

My winter life is summery, dark clouds cleared out,
hurting, painful memory storage bank shut out,
black, poisoned blood beached out, cleaned out,
forgiving, un-revenging heart opened out.

My winter life is summery; the sun shines
on and off with blues and reds, not from mines,
hidden minefields, but from the heart still struggling,
still fighting, still searching, with not much wailing.

My winter life is summery, feeling up the hill
trying not to cast, look down the hill
but viewing sunrise and sunset rays alike
with red and blue eyes alike.

My winter life is summery, my loveliest life!
Withered winter trees bring reborn summer life,
rejuvenated, hopeful, warm-blooded life,
spirited, enhanced, secure life.

My winter life is summery, although regretting
the love not received; never forgetting
the needy hands held out,
the bleeding heart cried for
the love and care, my summer due
always craved for.

27. My Future

My future is not bleak
'cause I'm not weak.
Past struggles have made me strong,
so my future shouldn't go wrong.

I've changed a lot,
blurred many a thing
I wrote in the past
in bleeding ink of dark red,

meaning and wishing
they will stay in the future
UNREAD.

My heart's future might feel them.
My brain's future should tear them.

My future is not bleak
'cause I'm not weak.
Past struggles have made me strong,
so my future shouldn't go wrong.

I've changed my thinking,
my outlook, my habits,
my ways of judging
my past hurts.

I don't want my future to resent,
avenge, judge, grudge, or lament
all that time lost in the past or present
in craving for love, relationship.

My future lies in my own life's ship,
built by myself despite with hardship,
not losing hopeful grip,
the key to surmount hardship.

My past is my behind.
I have a lot of it, by the way.
I don't want to look at my behind.

My future is in my front; there to stay
strong and well-shaped, leading the way.
I want to go ahead, not left behind.

My future is not bleak
'cause I'm not weak.
Past struggles have made me strong,
so my future shouldn't go wrong.

I want my future to be
carefree, worry-free,
judgment-free, resentment-free,
pain-free, guilt-free, remorse-free;

NOT smile-free, NOT laugh-free,
NOT joy-free.

Losing health in the future,
losing wealth in the future,
losing family members in the future,
losing close friends in the future,

reasons to be fretful, painful, stressful.
My trust in God will ever be helpful.

My future is not bleak
'cause I'm not weak.
Past struggles have made me strong,
so my future shouldn't go wrong.

SECTION V

On Lessons to Share

28. My Magical Experience

Magic is everywhere
around me, underneath me,
above me, all over me.

Sometimes I find it
in the wonders of nature,
sometimes, in facts of life,

sometimes, in my gains
sometimes, in my losses,
sometimes, in my failures.

Sometimes I look for it
in the mysterious
supernatural powers.

Sometimes it comes to me in prose,
in my readings and in my writings.
Sometimes it catches me unawares
in my mysterious dreams.

Sometimes it comes in lyrics and poems
which is what I am sharing with my readers.

29. Magic in Poetry

There is magic in poetry.
Poets can tell both truths
and lies in poetry,
never mind they believe or disbelieve.

Poets can fall in love in poetry,
never mind they love or not.

Poets can have sex in poetry,
even when they don't have partners,
and even with fair-skinned men,
even when the poet is
a dark-skinned female.

Poets can be saintly, holy,
or divine in their poetry.
Never mind they are just human,
prone to sin.

Poets can fight wars and break treaties
even when they truly love peace.

Poets can play tricks in poetry
much better than a magician's wand.

Poetry is not the magician's bag of tricks
for momentary, transient fun and display.

Poetry offers its own inspirational,
mysterious magic,
an everlasting, immortal experience
to both poets and readers.

Writing poetry is a magical experience.
I have to wait for the muse, though,
and give it permission
to play its magical tricks on me.

30. Poetry and Poets

Poetry is multilingual,
multicultural, multiracial.

Poetry speaks languages
of emotions, feelings,
visions, apparitions,
ambitions, expectations,
observations, and experiences

of varied
individuals, personalities,
cultures, nationalities,
religions, ethics, moralities,
and even immoralities;

provoking, evoking,
challenging, fighting,
crying, deploring,
cursing, blessing,
hoping, loving, caring,

imagining, fanaticizing, romanticizing,
walking, running, cruising, flying.

Poetry knows no discrimination.

Naked, clothed, covered, uncovered,
married, separated, divorced,
co-educated, cohabited,
young, old, single, widowed,

homosexual, bisexual, heterosexual,
transgender, transsexual,
monogamous, polygamous,
straights, gays, lesbians,

glorious, inglorious,
ethicists, atheists, agnostics, religious,
aliens, extraterrestrials,
sinners, divinities,

all have free entry
in disguised or revealed voice
into the majestic realm of poetry.

&&

Poems are mighty words
with power to translate all worlds,

past, present,
and future worlds,
living, dead, born,
and unborn worlds,

seen and unseen worlds,
personal, interpersonal,
and general worlds,
transcending all borders,
all handicaps, all disabilities,
all labeling, all taboos.

Poets don't have
to take board exams,
no multiple choice tests,
neither, any road tests.

Licensing themselves!

Nobody can contest
the poet's license.

My bullet-proof license!
My divine poetic license!

I carry it in my brain and heart,
not in my wallet, bag, or cart.

Oh! The freedom to be free!

31. My Dream Spirit

Dream, the invisible mighty spirit,
the possible-made-impossible spirit,
the impossible-made-possible spirit.
You are my illogical spirit!

You bed with me uninvited,
twice most every night
when I have my REM sleep.

Once I wake up
you stay out even at night;
not being ousted,
await my next REM sleep.

You've spirited me to
win and lose,
love and hate,
laugh and cry,

curse and bless,
hope and despair,
relive my pain and suffering,
make out with boyfriends,

inherit wealthy kingdoms,
aim high and reach low,
be happy and sad,
be sexy, sensual, sexual,

be enthroned queen,
get elected president,
be deposed, too,
be burned in purgatory,

also lit bright in eternal flame,
enjoying glorious beatitude.

I've had all my emotions
gotten loose in my dreams.

Surely, they're not my brain's
deliberate, planned activities.

Subconscious brain's realm
is unconscious dream's realm.

32. Dream

A dream
is just a dream,
an imperceptible spirit,
a stay-in-and-out spirit.

Naked eyes can't see it,
hands can't hold it.
Arms can't hug it,
lips can't kiss it.

Dreams live in the dream world
not in the corporeal world.

My real world is what I make,
not what my dreams make.

33. Passionate Romance

Cupid, the sporty boy,
the mischievous, playful archer
pulls his toy's string,
shoots his golden arrow
just for fun and merriment.

Frisky hit and run,
Cupid's right and privilege.
Chance and luck, lovers' wait line.

Lucky hearts pierced, punctured,
love's honeyed venom injected.
Fabulous input, phenomenal output!
Passion, Romance, Passionate Romance!

Eyes flame, lips protrude,
faces glow, necks extend,
hands quake, feet shake,
veins fill up, arteries charge,
bodies touch, souls feel,

sun descends, moon ascends.
Passion, Passion, Passion!
Romance, Romance, Romance!

Intellect fades, passion blooms.
Ecstatic, euphoric, paradisiacal,
culmination, consummation.
Surely, temporal and spiritual.

Passion, Romance, Passionate Romance!

Romance, the cosmic culture,
the global entertainment theater!

Once the door opens,
all play the same drama,
adding own music and drum
just for taste and variety.

Romance,
the universal actor,
the amusing performer!

34. Love

Some are born *to* love.
No matter what hurdles
cross or crisscross.

With or without money,
rewarded or not rewarded.
Call it instinctive love.
Nature's blessed gift!

Some are born
to *be* loved.

Adorned and adored,
chased and hunted,
forgiven and absolved,
sinned or not sinned.

Some *achieve* love
by hook or by crook,
well versed in
all the tricks to play.

All rules of love
observed and violated.
Envied and admired
by friends
and foes alike.

Some have love
thrust upon them.
No choice
but to love.

Bound by money, power,
wealth, or prestige.
Realistic at times,
Unrealistic otherwise.

Love can never be defined,
Parsed, or analyzed.

All the world is love,
all the lovers acting
the one and only
sweet four-letter word
used and abused!

35. Success

Success is your hard-earned reward
not measured against money values.
not quantified in price values.

Your own award to yourself,
won with no external evaluation,
no rating or scoring,
no bell curve grading,
no comparison and contrast.

Would winning the lotto help?
Would global leadership count?
Would world renown count?
Would rich inheritance help?

Your own answer to yourself
would always be of help.

What you make of life
is judged by your own standards.
Low, medium, high doesn't matter.

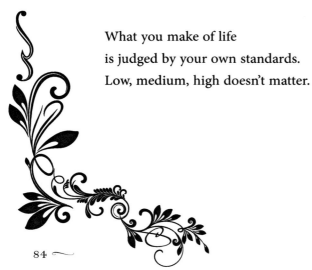

Accepting yourself
is the only key
that opens the door to success.

Sleep guilt-free at night?
Get up in the morning with hopes?
Take up challenges on the way?
Accept failures without falls?
Go ahead with zest?
You ARE successful.

❧❧

A hard-to-practice dictum,
my aim in life all through.

36. The Power of Superstitions

You the irrational king
ruling over my rational intellect!

I know you lack reason and intelligence.
I know, as a human
I have super-intelligence over you.

But I do not know why I let you into
my super-intellectual dominion,
giving you freedom to enslave me!

You trick me with your magic;
you hypnotize me with
your-brand narcotic drugs,
inducing dull sleep into
my intelligent brain.

You mesmerize me
with your mystic air,
clouding my rational thoughts.

You blindfold my brain's eye,
changing my vision from real to unreal,
natural to unnatural, genuine to grotesque,
legitimate to illegitimate, true to untrue,
godly to devilish, religious to irreligious.

You reign over kingdoms and superpowers;
fell mighty kings who challenge you.
Your invisible kingdom is mighty
with your constructive and destructive powers.
You manipulate to reign over our powers.

Soothsayers, fortune-tellers,
palm readers, witches,
the Oracle,
the evil eye,
the broken mirror,
left-foot bridal entry,
Friday the 13th, the 13th floor,
the Ides of March,
so goes your countless list.

Your weapons are legion.
You get free entry into
weak hearts and minds.

You don't discriminate.
Races, colors, cultures,
civilizations, nations,
all your equally treated victims!

37. Beauty's Dual-Power[1]

Standing on the ruins of Troy,
excavated, celebrated,
my thoughts wandered—

Men, women, gods, goddesses,
wars, soldiers,
kings, queens, princes, princesses,
beauty, passion, abduction, seduction,
shame, revenge, feuds, grace, disgrace,
pride, valor, adventure, loyalty, heroes,
warships, swords, arrows, spears, shields.

No heroines, no men slaves,
all women slaves!

All human vices and virtues,
all tools of might and power,
both of humans and of gods,

all epitomized, summarized, in
one woman's beauty power.

Helen of Sparta
turned into Helen of Troy,
and back into Helen of Sparta.

1.   This poem was written as a reflection on my visit to Turkey in November
      2010, when I got the opportunity to visit the excavated ruins of Troy.

"The woman whose face
launched a thousand ships!"[2]

The most beautiful woman of all times
unparalleled model of feminine beauty
adored, adorned, worshipped, coveted
desired, pursued, chased, by
the most powerful, gallant men
of all classes, status.

Beauty's radiance so strong, so mighty!

Abducted beauty emanates power;
Menelaus, the husband,
in kingly throne shakes,
made helpless, powerless,
by beauty power.

A challenge to male cultures
of all generations!

Walking around Troy l-IX[3]
thanks to Calvert, Schliemann,
Dörpfeld, Blegen, Korfmann,[4]
my thoughts wandered—

One woman—
holding for ever, never-to-be extinct,
unique, immortal place,

---

2. Quote from Christopher Marlowe's *Dr. Faustus*.
3. Refers to the sites excavated at different times.
4. Archeologists involved in the excavation of the ruins of Troy.

conferred, not acquired, not earned
by heroism, achievements,
or test scores.

Not won by competing or fighting
wars on her own grounds.

A gifted place granted gratis
by thousands of men
banded together, bound by oaths
that made them voluntarily fight, shed blood
for ten long years in the bloody battlefield.

Won the unique celebratory place in
history, literature, mythology, legend.

Homer, Virgil, Sophocles,
Euripides, Ovid, Aeschylus
Poe, Doolittle,

all sourced, generated
their themes, plots, characters
from one unique woman.

Trojan condoms, Trojan contraceptives,
Trojan games, Trojan computer virus,
Trojan horse politics,

apple of discord, Achilles heel
so goes the dictionary list.
All from one source, one woman!

Mounting on the replicated Trojan horse,[5]
sitting in the wooden horse's belly,
simulating the Achaean soldiers hidden,
my thoughts wandered—

Trojan horse, forerunner of
modern strategic wars and murders,
seeming symbol of peace turned into
evil lurking behind,
meant for doom, destruction.

❧❧

Beauty is indefinable,
though describable,
is inspirational, mystical,
mysterious, spiritual.

Is meant for truth, harmony,
accord, not discord.

5. The story of the Trojan horse is told in Virgil's *The Aeneid*. It was a strategy used
    by the Greeks to end the ten-year-old Trojan War. The Greeks built a wooden
    horse in the belly of which hid thirty soldiers. The Greeks pretended to sail back,
    when the Trojans pulled the horse into the city as a victory trophy. The soldiers
    hidden in the horse came out and opened the gates for the rest of the
    Greek army to enter.

Is lovable, adorable,
though viciously tempting, too.

War fought for land,
wealth, and women
is anything but beauty.

Why can't men be
happy and content
with whatever beauty
they've won already?

38. The World Theater Power

All the world is a theater
with seats reserved,
restricted, ranked, ordered,
prepaid, prearranged.

Gender power, racial power,
political power, religious power,
class power, caste power,
family power, tribal power,
status power, skin color power,
so goes the list of ranked power.

The world theater power!

All powerless, standbys!

Not excluded are those
even with talents and merits,
who happen to wait forever
for both shows and seats
in the world theater power.

Long-term struggles and conflicts,
fights for rights and claims,
could sometimes bring in benefits

and win seats
for the powerless
in the world theater power.

39. Anger, the Virus

Anger, the virus, infests us,
once we open the entrance door
of frustration, worries, fear,
hatred, or any hurtful emotions.

Attacking our
emotional immune system
it could storm, thunder,
cloudburst, or snow.

No curative antibiotic pills, though,
except love, patience, quietude,
and most of all,

FORGIVING,
the best antidote.

Anger is animalistic.
It doesn't pay to be angry.

Humanity would be
better off
without this
destructive faculty.

40. Change and Rebirth

All the leaves that fall
and die in the fall
will come back to life
in the spring,
sprouting from
the rooted roots.

Roots give life.
Be well-rooted.

Lives that get uprooted
could get re-rooted,
renewed, renovated,
replenished, rejuvenated
in enhanced soil,

giving birth to new lives,
new harvests.

Seasons change,
nature's hues change,
life's cycles change,
societies change,
individuals change.

Face the inevitable change.

Change to be reborn,
change for the better,
enjoy the rebirth.

My lifelong desire!

41. Forgiving

Pay heed, mature hearts!

The road ahead may not be long.
Secure the path by stretching long,
not with vengeful, hateful thoughts,
but with concerned, forgiving thoughts.

Forgiving revitalizes body parts,
warms up blood in frozen hearts.

Opt for forgiving,
the best noninvasive surgery
for all stricken hearts.

Get love's blocks bypassed,
feverish, hateful arteries surpassed.

Miraculous cure for paining hearts!
New blood, new life, new starts!

42. Hope

Hope. The invisible,
indubitable presence
felt and experienced
on and off, with offers
of assurance, confidence.

Never-starting, never-ending,
never-fading, never-dying
incandescent, eternal
beacon light.

Never to lose sight of,
always to look at.
Bought with no cost,
ever rewarded with rebate.

43. Memories

Memories...
all life's experiences,
all life's data pleasant and unpleasant
from the time we can remember,
filed, stored, encoded in the brain.

What to decode is your own
conscious decision,
no matter even the unconscious
has access to all the cells
of this memory storage.

Wisdom dictates not to decode any
with the purpose to blame the past.

Your past is a written history book.
Since only you know the codes,
you can block and lock the shelves
using your own codes.

If ever you choose
to unlock the shelves,
to open and read
this memory book,

make sure you tear off
all the red, bleeding pages,

write new pages,
translating and transforming
the wisdom gained from
new experiences
and mature growth

into lessons of new learning
for future reading.

Don't let painful memories
torment your brain.

Keep yourself sane and serene,
standing tall against all odds
and picking up fragments
of pleasant memories.

Rebuild life on pleasurable experiences.
Light the memory lane in bright colors.

Move on to make new memories
fashioned by your mature dreams.

Future should be positive shape-ups,
not based on past negative build-ups,
despite destiny being
not always in your own hands.

44. The Future

Focus on the future in front;
the past is to forgive, not to confront.
Let the past dwell behind, not facing the front.
Don't ever let it make a trip to the front.

The past is spilt milk.
No use to cry over all that's gone.
Learn from mistakes made, but gone.

Hold fast to the future.
It may or may not last long.
Keep it close to heart to mature,
making its spirit ever strong.

Change, not letting change
stay in the present.
Be reborn into the future,
shaped out of the present,
the time for the future.

Live the present in full; create the future.
NOW is the only and only time for the future.

SECTION VI

On a Keepsake

45. My Electric Frying Pan

Why do I keep this
once used and overused
stainless steel electric pan?

Now in honor kept
with care and respect,
but never used at all.

Once my sole kitchen tool,
my broiler, my oven,
my toaster, my egg beater
my kettle, etc....

Never given away to charity
with other bric-a-brac
in big chunky bags.

Always moved with me
in a nicely packed box
from borough to borough.

Manhattan, Brooklyn
Queens, now in the Bronx.

My live-in companion,
my kitchen medallion,
my keepsake, my souvenir,

telling and retelling
stories and anecdotes of
my uprooted beginning
in a foreign country,

which now is
my dearly loved
adopted, adored
home country.

Oh, my good old
Electric Frying Pan!

Cherished and treasured
over and above
my modern kitchen,
where you now sit
with all due dignity
for ever and ever....

SECTION VII

On Nature's Beauty

46. Ode to Hudson-on-the-Cliffs[1]

Oh, my Hudson-on-the Cliffs!
Panoramic, "Riveramic" view!
My eyes' pleasing hue!

You give birth
to crazy dreams to cross
not over the bridge[2] across,
driving Mercedes-Benz,
but just to swim across
in bare, see-through swim suits,

not to miss the love-scenes,
the lusty, wealthy kisses
of the Palisades lovers,
dating and waiting.

I dream floating on you
with big trade ships
pulled by small tug-boats.

Small wonders!
Big highlights!
Great views!

1. This poem was inspired by the Hudson River and the cliiffs that run along it,
   called New Jersey Palisades or Hudson Palisades. I have a good view of the river
   and the cliffs from my apartment.
2. George Washington Bridge, the suspension bridge which spans the Hudson
   River, connecting New York City and New Jersey.

You sure are
seasonal in all seasons,
fresh feasts to my bosom!

Luscious spring
on the Cliffs-over-Hudson!

Luxuriant, lustrous,
St. Patrick's green,[3]
watered, mirrored,
spiritual, saintly,
inspirational.

Summer on the Hudson
is playful,
youthful, lively, lovely,
full of romance,
sensual, sensuous.

Pleasure boats, leisure boats
with couples, lovers,
in passionate embrace.

3. Refers to the green color, especially the green shamrocks and ribbons worn on St. Patrick's Day, in honor of St. Patrick, recognized as the patron saint of Ireland. St. Patrick's Day is celebrated internationally on the 17th of March, especially in the Irish Diaspora, including the U.S.

Columbia Baker Field's[4]
row-boats, race boats,
competing to win,
to be the first
in Hudson-on-the Cliffs.

Fall foliage
wraps you in rainbows,
clothes you in Joseph's robe.[5]
Vermont
In Hudson-on-the Cliffs.

Clouds above
peep in and out,
hide and seek,
all in envy
and in shame.

No dead black winter
no aches and pains,
no suffering,
no sad thoughts,
no laments,

4. Refers to Columbia University's Baker Athletics Complex for outdoor sports programs,
    which features a boathouse, in addition to several stadiums, such as those for soccer,
    hockey, etc. I enjoy watching the rowing teams practicing rowing their boats in
    their uniform outfits.
5. Refers to the story of Joseph, one of the 12 sons of Jacob, who received the gift of a
    multicolored robe from his father as a symbol of his special love for him
    (Gen.37: 3 [K J]). This story became the theme for Andrew Lloyd Webber's
    musical, "Joseph and the Amazing Technicolor Dream Coat," with lyrics from
    Tim Rice, winner of the Academy, Golden Globe, Tony, and Grammy awards.

no sorrows,
In the winter
In Hudson-on-the Cliffs.

Marble ice of odd colors
black, white, grey "glaciers,"
polluted from air above,
and sewage underneath
surf on the waves,
waving in the winds.

Joseph's robe,
another kind!

In the winter
In Hudson-on-the Cliffs.

Give me wings
to fly and flutter,
hover and linger.

A boon to carry your
spring in my hand,
fall in my heart,
summer in my eyes,
winter on my lips.

47. Ode to the Evening Sky

Oh! The radiant evening sky!

I love to watch your beaming light
when you shine over the cliffs,
with the orange globe set
and hidden behind the Palisades.

Oh! The luminous, lustrous,
luscious evening sky!

I see your powerful rays
spread across and above the cliffs,
painting the evening horizon
in your lively colors.

Silvery white, golden yellow,
with soft grey linings,
crimson-red, with mellow
wavy, light trimmings.

Unrivaled, uniquely glorious,
so different, so wondrous!

Oh! The heavenly glowing, lusty sky!

Come, embrace me all evening.
Hold me close, kiss my neck,

my cheeks, and lips too, if you like.
Move my outfit off my shoulders,
clothe me in your colorful evening gown.
I love to be cuddled up, fondled, too.

Light me up,
my biological clock is ticking;
I am in the evening of my life.
I need all your evening warmth.
I love your evening glamor.

Your peace and tranquillity
add spice to the evening of my life.

I am sad when I see you waning
fading and fading,
finally disappearing,
with dark clouds overtaking.

The evening of my life is slowly waning,
and I will disappear one day.
But like you, I will reappear
in another world on another day.

In Elysium, Paradise,
The eternal Pacific and Atlantic together!

48. Ode to Autumn

Autumn, my most favorite season of all
the crown prince of the year.

I love you for the multi-colored blanket
you wrap me in.
Red, gold, purple, brown, green.

I know you do not bloom
but you groom my heart with colors;
and I am pleased and happy with that.

I do not miss the summer fragrance
when I see your leaves of variant hues.

Your touch is soft, cool, kind.
I can go out and enjoy the world
with just a jacket over my light clothes,
walk around, keeping you in mind.

Oh, sweet autumn,
I love to breathe in your cool air.

You make me feel young,
you balance my heart's rhythm,
you tickle me with your soothing air.

Your fruit harvest is delicious to taste,
your colorful leaves are amorous to feel.

You bring me capital gain
of what I lose in the spring;[1]
an hour of precious sleep,
a gain for the fiscal year
which I am glad
I do not have to report
to Uncle Sam.[2]

I do not want to call you fall.
Your name is autumn, not fall.

You do not make me fall
like my many a cruel winter fall.

I miss you, darling,
when you fall and die,
giving way to winter,
the cruel monster whom I hate.

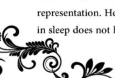

1. Refers to the "daylight saving time" observed in most parts of the Northern
    Hemisphere, which has given rise to the phrase "spring forward, fall back." It
    requires one to set the clock forward one hour at the beginning of spring and back
    one hour in fall.
2. Refers to the U.S. government's personification, originally a cartoon
    representation. Here, it is a humorous, poetic statement that the one-hour of gain
    in sleep does not have to be reported on the tax form to be filed each year.

I know for sure
you will be born again the next year.
I have hope in you, for sure,
though you fall every year.

If I were a bird, I would fly to you,
share your cozy, colorful nest,
fall on you, dwell in with you,
and sleep with you
in your cool nest.

SECTION VIII

On Supernatural Powers

49. To Archangel Gabriel[1]

Archangel Gabriel, pay me a visit, please.
I know I'm not a virgin, like Virgin Mary[2]
whom you loved to be God's messenger to.

While Mary was born
to be a virgin all her life
I wasn't, as you know very well.
I don't hanky-panky, anyhow,
so don't you think I deserve
a visitation from you?

I pray that you appear to me,
revealing to me
in clear terms
what it looks like to be
up there above.

---

1. Archangels are believed to be messengers of God to humans. Belief in angels exists in Judaic, Christian, and Islamic traditions. The Hebrew Bible has references to the archangel Gabriel (Dan. 8: 15–26). Angel Gabriel is mentioned three times in the Qur'an, and is believed to have appeared to Muhammad and revealed the sacred book. According to both Islamic and Christian traditions, Gabriel was the one who visited both Zachariah and Mary to announce the births of John the Baptist, Christ's cousin, (Lk.1: 10-17[KJ & NAB])and of Christ respectively (Lk. 1:26–38 [KJ & NAB]). In all three religions (Jewish, Christian, and Islamic), Gabriel is considered the angel of revelation.
2. In both Islamic and Christian tradition, Mary conceived Jesus miraculously while remaining a virgin (Matt. 1:18-25, Lk. 1:26-34 [KJ & NAB]). It is also believed that she remained a virgin even after she gave birth to Jesus.

Hopefully, I'll win the victory,[3]
and fly up to live with you.
I believe I deserve to be rewarded
for all my earthly suffering, pain,
sacrifices, and altruism
in my life down below.

Please reveal to me, Archangel,
what kind of food, the fruit of
my earthly life's victory
I'll have up there above.

I don't want the manna,[4] though.
Why should I wake up
early in the morning,
rush out to collect it
before the Sun god
makes his appearance?

Once I am up there,
I want to rest forever.

3. "To those who win the victory, I will give the right to eat from the fruit of the tree of life that grows in the Garden of God" (Rev. 2:18 [NAB]).

4. Manna was the food God provided to the Israelites at one of their campsites during their exodus from Egypt (Exod.16: 13-36 [NAB]). It was available to them six days every week. "Morning after morning, they gathered it till each had enough to eat; but when the sun grew hot, the manna melted (Exod.16: 21 [NAB]).

What I really want you
to reveal to me is
if I can get ambrosia[5] up there,
the anti-aging celestial food,
which I've heard rumored down here,
all the divinities up there eat.

Please bring Athena[5] with you.
I want her to give me some ambrosia
while I am still down here,
exactly as she did to
Penelope[5] in her sleep,
so my senior skin will be stripped off
from all signs of aging,
glow with youthful divine radiance,

and when I reach up there,
all handsome men already up there
would burn with passion
at the very sight of me,
vie with each other to court me,

5.   In Greek mythology, ambrosia and nectar are used interchangeably as the divinities'
      food and drink, the key to their immortal youth. Athena, the goddess of wisdom,
      is believed to have given ambrosia to Penelope, Ulysses's wife, and stripped her
      off all wrinkles and other apparent signs of aging from her skin in order to make
      her look attractive to her suitors.

But I will make my own choice,
fooling the men! Great fun!!

Please reveal to me
if I can also get the nectar,
the intoxicating
Olympian honey drink.

Down here I can't revel intoxicated
because I fear the consequences.

I don't want to tarnish my A+ report card
which I now have on record.

Archangel Gabriel, you know
I was born and brought up in India,
so I expect you to reveal to me
that I'll sure get amrita,[6]

the nectar of the Indian gods and goddesses,
not anything spicy hot, though
which I have a lot down here,
but the honey sweet, transcendental fluid,
which I have heard,
helps the Indian deities stay immortal.

I want to be a little Indian
Cinderella immortalized.

6.   In Hindu mythology, Amrita is the equivalent of Greek ambrosia and nectar.

Finally, let me be serious.

Please reveal to me, Archangel Gabriel,

how I can, in my worldly garden down here,

which I want to be

the same as the garden of God,

grow the divine plants,

yielding not any manna,

but the anti-aging,

anti-oxidant ambrosia,

the intoxicating nectar, and

the immortality-inducing amrita.

I claim my right to be immortalized!

50. Angels

Where do all the angels dwell?
True, some dwell in heaven's realm
with their King and His entourage.

True, some come down on
the King's own mission,
command, and permission
to serve humans with no intermission.

Also true, there are angels on earth's realm.
Some are gone despite wanting to dwell
here back home with their homey entourage.

They leave without asking permission,
having done their mission
though with some intermission.

Angels come into my realm
at intervals and with intermission,
announcing their mission
with or without my permission.

They always want to dwell
in my world with no entourage.

Some are now in heaven's realm
with sky their assigned home to dwell in
with all fellow stars their entourage.

They have my permission.
I know for sure about their mission
to watch me with no intermission.

Don't they want to come down to dwell
here, leave their kingly realm,
stay with me with God's own entourage?

They don't have His permission,
being assigned to do their mission
to flash light on me with no intermission.

I see where all my vanished angels dwell.
I see them dwelling as stars in the sky's vast realm.
Guarding me is still their mission
with other glittering torches their entourage.

I wish they had permission
to come down at some intermission!
Look, I'm still down here in my own realm
with finished and unfinished mission
still doing and undoing with no intermission!

SECTION IX
On A Personal Loss

51. To Thankachan,[1] my Big Fan from Annie, your Dearest Wife
February 14, 2003 (Valentine's Day)[2]

My best friend
the best of best friends!

Always proud of me
and all my achievements
in academe
and community.

You shared my surfing
up and down,
down and up
sailing with me
my academic ship.

My big, big fan!
Trumpeting my halos
louder and louder,
ever to be heard
by all the world
all around you.

---

1. My husband's nickname. His official first name was Mathew.
2. Mathew died on February 10. On the second day of wake held in honor of him, which coincided with Valentine's Day, I read out this poem at the funeral home crowded with family members, relatives, and friends.

Keep singing
in the glory of heaven
with all the angels and saints
your favorite hymn
"Annie, my wife, is great."

And I'll sing the chorus
"Thankachan, my husband,
was my greatest fan
down here on earth
and still is my fan
up there
in heaven above."

SECTION X

On A 9/11 Loss

52. In Celebration of Valsa Raju's Memory

Valsa, you lived and loved
true to your name
sweet and lovely.

Valsa, the delightful
you, the youthful,
colorful, powerful,
skillful, cheerful.

You "pumped love and courage,
hope and confidence
into friends and family alike,"
in Raju's[1] own words.

Your ambition knew no bounds;
your works put no stops to
your skills-on-the-move, with dreams
to climb the rungs and ladders
of professions and corporations.

Strong-willed, goal-filled,
assertive, competitive,
and cooperative, too.

Full of trust in God,
with roots in religion,
with no Sundays missed,
anchored in family values.

1.   Valsa's husband

"True and faithful wife,"
so says Raju.
"Caring, sharing, helping,
and teaching mom,"
so says Sonia.

Spouse, housewife,
handywoman and handyman alike
chef, mother, financier, stockbroker,
counselor, employer and employee
investor and investment
all in one.

Multiple jobs,
multiple burdens, too.

You climbed up the social ladder,
winning all the time,
thriving in your immigrant land,
the land of
different tongues and tastes.

Didn't have to complete
two-score-year span
to fill and fulfill
your cup of goals.

Your American dreams realized!

Suburban cozy house,
six-figure paychecks,
cars and comforts,
all left for Sonia and Sanjay.[2]

A model immigrant
for all hyphenated Americans,
all aspiring women
of all races and creeds.

Your tree of labor and valor
grows and blossoms ever
as real as your flowers of gift
to Sonia and Sanjay who walk
your trail of glory
honor, merit,
values, and ethics.

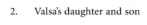

Terrorists can never burn your dreams.
No terror can frighten your spirit.

2.   Valsa's daughter and son

SECTION XI

On Being American

53. Only in America[1]

Perseverance counts, skills count.
Rags to riches, only in America.

Homeless, spouseless, singles, all in count
dropouts, orphans, in count
immigrants, refugees, all in count
grew up in one-room log cabins, sure in count
in tenements, of course, in count.

Where you start doesn't count in America.
Where you end counts in America.

Perseverance counts, skills count
Rags to riches, only in America.

1. Quote from Christopher Gardner, whose life story gave rise to the movie,
    "Pursuit of Happyness" (2006), starring Will Smith, winner of Academy,
    Golden Globe, and Grammy awards.

54. Immigrant American

Immigrants from many a nationality
making racial groups of diversity
ethnic groups of modernity
religious groups of spirituality.

Hands together, held together
one umbrella spread forever.

No values lost, all gained.
New ideas, new agendas, all organized.
Relentless work, the key maintained.
Visibility, the goal shared.

Your name is Immigrant American.

Keep your name, spread your fame.
Fight your cause, be American.

Mighty force dwells in your name,
AMERICAN!

SECTION XII

On Indian-Americans

55. Indian-American Pioneers[1]

Past, present, future, all combined;
cultures, religions, castes, classes,
all collected, mixed, developed
into one entity in the new land.

Reborn into the new name,
Indian-American.

Worthy pioneers, achievers.
Be proud of your success!

Winners are you all.
Gems in the crowns
of Indian-American settlers
in the United States.

You came with ambitions
filled to your cups' brims,
burning with passions
and aspirations,
raveled and unraveled,
and with dreams so inspired.

Worthy achievers!
You groaned with labor pains,

1.   Refers to the builders of the Indian-American immigrant society in the U.S.,
      which I am proud to be a member of, and which is currently one of the most
      economically successful ethnic groups in the U.S.

pushing, pushing, and pushing,
moving, moving, and moving,
until the fruit of your labors
was born to future generations.

You struggled to root
your uprooted root.

Strong and sturdy
the tree is growing steady.
Solid, secure, well-rooted,
born, reborn, well-nourished.

You've toiled so hard,
sacrificed, suffered, struggled,
to climb the mosaic ladder,
the American dream ladder.

With education, your beacon light,
work ethics, your navigator,
you're now anchored, well-moored
on the shore of your dream land,
now your real land,
AMERICA!

Pioneers, achievers!
Pains never forgotten,
but discounted are they all now
to count only the gains and profits.

Pat your back,
all you achievers.

You've left all the gates open,
wide open,
for our worthy children
to get in freely
and live in comfort
in their birth land,
AMERICA!

SECTION XIII

On Young Indian-Americans

56. To Young Indian-Americans

Build your ship straight,[1] O my younger generation,
keep your lovely vessel strong and sturdy.
It shouldn't cry, but should only laugh at any disaster,
even when wrestling with waves and whirlwinds.

Listen to your heart's voice.
Let it not speak in vain.
Put your heart in your work, for the heart
gives grace to every art.

Build your ship straight, O my younger generation,
every heart, every mind, and brain
should bring its power to nurture and share
and help build your ship's walls with care.

Choose the timbers with greatest care.
Beware of all that is unsound.
Remember, only what is sound and strong
should belong to your vessel.

Make your vessel fair and beautiful
Fondle her in your arms
with tenderness and watchful hearts.
Let her set sail, leaping into the ocean deep.

1.   This poem is an adaptation of H.W. Longfellow's
     "The Building of the Ship."

Gentleness, love, and trust
prevail o'er angry wave and gust.

We, your forerunners' tears, fears
and all our prayers, hopes
are all for you.
Sure, are all for you.

Build your ship straight, O my younger generation,
keep your lovely vessel strong and sturdy.
It shouldn't cry, but should only laugh at any disaster,
even when wrestling with all waves and whirlwinds.

SECTION XIV

On My Old Story

57. When I Am Gone...

In a short or long time I am going to be
an old story written by me,
not as a love sonnet but as an epic
of Herculean[1] heroic dimensions.

The epic poem
Of my daring, precarious journey,
of my life's navigation
in the tempestuous ocean tide
between Scylla and Charybdis.[2]

When I am gone...
do not let my epic die.

Remember,
I kept on writing it
all my life,
never taking a break.

---

1. Refers to Hercules, who is considered the greatest of Greek heroes and known for having successfully performed twelve seemingly impossible tasks.

2. In Greek tradition, these are two dangerous sea monsters (Scylla, in the shape of a six-headed rock, and Charybdis, a whirlpool), situated at the strait of Messina between Sicily and the Italian mainland. Navigating the ships in this strait meant choosing between two risky situations—hence, the phrase "between Scylla and Charybdis." Odysseus, in Homer's *Odyssey*, is described to have chosen to sail through Scylla because he preferred to lose some of his sailors to losing the entire ship caught in the whirlpool. The message here is to choose the lesser of the evils, when faced with nothing but insurmountable problems.

When I am gone...
look for my legacy
in the epic I am leaving.

Models and examples
of how I fought to live with diligence,
with passionate love to live,
with singular aim and devotion
to achieve and succeed
against all odds at all times.

When I am gone...
do not let my epic die.

Remember,
I kept on writing it
all my life,
never taking a break.

When I am gone...
Look up my epic

in the encyclopedia of

Risky Ventures,
Commitment and Loyalty,
Altruism and Sacrifice,
Pain with Endurance
and Resilience,
Patience, though with Anxiety,

Giving, not of receiving,
Action, not of words,
Hope, not of despair,
Forgiving, not of revenge.

When I am gone...
do not let my epic die.

Remember,
I kept on writing it
all my life,
never taking a break.

When I am gone...
I am not taking
my epic with me
for me to read.

I am leaving it behind
for all posterity to read
and copy.
No copyrights reserved!

When I am gone...
do not let my epic die.

Remember,
I kept on writing it
all my life,
never taking a break...

CPSIA information can be obtained at www.ICGtesting.com
Printed in the USA
BVOW011134040413

317310BV00002B/6/P